DOLAN, Edward F. *America in World War II: 1944.* 72p. maps. photos. bibliog. index. (America in World War II Series). CIP. Millbrook. 1993. PLB $15.90. ISBN 1-56294-221-2. LC 91-30808.

Gr 5-8—Dolan has added another fine title to this series. The introduction reviews the war as covered in the three previous volumes. The six chapters of eight to ten pages each describe the major campaigns of 1944. The European theater is covered in chronological order while the final chapter describes the war in the Pacific. The text reads easily. Virtually all photos are full-page; five are in color. The rest are archival; most of them have appeared in other publications. Small photos of leading figures are included. Four well-placed colorful maps coordinate well with the text. Combined with the previous books, this is an excellent introduction to World War II for this age level.—*Eldon Younce, Harper Elementary School, KS*

AMERICA IN WORLD WAR II

1944

AMERICA IN WORLD WAR II

EDWARD F. DOLAN

THE MILLBROOK PRESS
BROOKFIELD, CONNECTICUT

Cover photograph courtesy of the National Archives

Maps by Joe LeMonnier

All photographs courtesy of the National Archives,
except, the Library of Congress: pp. 41 and 44.

Published by The Millbrook Press
2 Old New Milford Road
Brookfield, Connecticut 06804

Library of Congress Cataloging-in-Publication Data

(Revised for vol. 4) Dolan Edward F., 1924–
America in World War II.

Includes bibliographical references and index.
Contents: —[3] 1943—[4] 1944
1. World War, 1939–1945—Campaigns—Juvenile
literature. 2. World War, 1939–1945—United
States—Juvenile literature. [1. World War, 1939–
1945—Campaigns. 2. World War, 1939–1945
—United States.] I. America in World War 2.
II. America in World War Two. III. Title.
D743.7.D65 1992 940.54'1 91-30808
ISBN 1-56294-221-2 (v. [4])

CONTENTS

INTRODUCTION: THE STORY THUS FAR

The United States was plunged into World War II on December 7, 1941, when Japan unleashed surprise air attacks against six U.S. military installations on the Hawaiian island of Oahu. Chief among those bases was the giant Pearl Harbor naval base. Hours later, U.S. bases on the Philippine Islands and the islands of Wake, Guam, and Midway were bombed. Also hit were British targets along the Pacific edge of Asia.

The attacks marked the latest step in Japan's campaign to become the most powerful nation in Asia. That campaign dated back to 1931, when Japan invaded northern China. China had been fighting the Japanese ever since.

On December 8, 1941, an angry United States declared war on Japan. Japan's allies—Germany and Italy—then declared war on America. The United States answered with a return declaration of war. Great Britain, which was already at war with Germany and Italy, joined America in the fight with Japan. The European conflict had erupted in 1939, when German dictator Adolf Hitler invaded Poland, after which he overran Belgium, Luxembourg, Holland, and France.

The chief Allied leaders —Soviet premier Joseph Stalin, U.S. president Franklin Roosevelt, and British prime minister Winston Churchill— met late in 1943 to plan war strategy.

(The terms *Allies* and *Allied* were used in the war to denote the nations fighting Germany, Italy, and Japan. Those three countries were known as the *Axis Powers.*)

In the final weeks of 1941, Japanese troops captured Wake and Guam. The first months of 1942 saw them invade the Philippines and take control of the islands.

But 1942 was not a complete disaster for America. The factories at home began to produce all the materials that would be needed to win the war. Then, in June, the United States recorded a major victory in the Pacific. An American fleet seriously crippled the Japanese Navy when the enemy attempted to take the island of Midway, far to the north of Hawaii.

The victory showed that the Americans were regaining their strength after being hurt at Pearl Harbor and were ready to drive the enemy back to Japan. That drive began in late 1942 and raged on through 1943 as the Americans took a series of Japanese-held islands in the South Pacific, among them New Guinea, the Solomons, and Tarawa.

Far across the world, 1943 saw three major actions. First, starting in late 1942, British and U.S. forces invaded North Africa to drive the Germans out of Morocco, Algeria, and Tunisia, a job that was completed by May 1943. Next, the two forces crossed the Mediterranean Sea and took the island of Sicily near the southwestern tip of Italy. Finally, they invaded Italy itself.

Italy dropped out of the war, but the German forces there continued to fight on. Slowly, the Allies battled northward in an effort to clear the country of the enemy.

At year's end, they came up to the series of German fortifications known as the Gustav Line. . . .

ONE: THE WAR IN ITALY

The Gustav Line ran through a mountainous region that extended across the width of Italy about a hundred miles south of the nation's capital, Rome. Here, on rocky slopes, the Germans had embedded their artillery, built steel bunkers, turned caves into machine-gun nests, and concealed their tanks inside peasant huts.

And here, at the close of 1943, they waited to meet and finally crush the two forces that had been driving them north since invading Italy last September. The two were the U.S. 5th Army, commanded by Lieutenant General Mark Clark, and the British 8th Army, under General Sir Bernard Law Montgomery. Heading the entire Italian campaign was America's Lieutenant General Dwight D. Eisenhower. He had commanded the Allied armies in this area of the world since their invasion of North Africa in 1942.

On arriving at the Gustav Line, the two Allied armies were eager to surge past it so that they could move on to Rome as quickly as possible. They were certain that, once Rome fell, the Germans would realize that all was lost in Italy and give up the fight there.

But, for weeks, the job of getting past the Line proved impossible. The firmly entrenched German troops threw back every attack. For example, a U.S. attempt to cross a river near the western edge of the Line in January 1944 ended in disaster when enemy machine-gun and artillery fire blasted the Americans from almost point-blank range. One U.S. unit started across with 187 men and came back with 17.

The 5th Army faced a particularly difficult obstacle about midway along the Line—Monte Cassino, a 1,700-foot-high mountain of rock. Standing atop it was a monastery that had been founded in A.D. 529 by Saint Benedict. Military experts had long called Monte Cassino, with its steep walls and narrow trails, the "perfect fortress."

It seemed to be a perfect fortress in late 1943 and the first days of 1944 as the 5th Army troops tried to reach the crest, with their every attempt failing. One effort saw the Americans battle their way up Cassino's rock-strewn face for three long weeks before finally being thrown back just four hundred yards from the top.

GENERAL MARK CLARK

His U.S. 5th Army fought throughout the Italian campaign. During the campaign, the 5th became an "international army." Joining its American troops were fighters of twenty-six nationalities. Among them were Canadian, New Zealand, Polish, Yugoslav, Greek, north and south African, Brazilian, and Italian soldiers.

THE ATTACK AT ANZIO ▪ Stopped in their every try to break through the Line, the Allies turned to a new tactic. They decided to slip around its side, get behind it, and weaken its defenders by cutting off their supply line from the cities to its north.

And so, on January 22, 1944, a force of 37,000 U.S. and British troops boarded ships that sailed up the Tyrrhenian Sea under the cover of darkness and put them ashore on the beaches at the small fishing village of Anzio. In the next days, their number would rise to 50,000.

The assault caught the Germans by surprise, and the landing was made without trouble. The attackers were now to spear inland and cut a major supply highway that ran from Rome to the Line. But the Germans, though surprised, reacted with lightning speed. While the invaders were still spreading out along the beaches, eight enemy divisions came rushing in and blocked the path to the highway.

The Allied troops found themselves caught in a steel trap as the enemy surrounded the three inland sides of the Anzio

A Nazi shell explodes on the beach at Anzio, narrowly missing an amphibious craft bringing supplies to the Allied troops trapped there.

FIELD MARSHAL ALBERT KESSELRING

Kesselring commanded the German troops in the Italian campaign. It was due to his fast action that eight German divisions rushed to Anzio in time to trap the American invaders on the beaches.

beaches. They dug in and remained on the marshy beaches for four months. All the while, crouching in damp foxholes, they were relentlessly shelled by the Germans.

Meanwhile, the assaults on the Gustav Line continued. On February 15, 225 Allied bombers hit Monte Cassino, leveling the monastery atop it. Then, pressing through rubble so thick that it had to be pushed aside by bulldozers before the troops could move, the 5th again attacked. The fighting that followed took place in such close quarters that there was no room for the medics from either side to reach the wounded. At times, the 5th's men had to battle their way from floor to floor through mountainside buildings. In the end, the Germans clung stubbornly to their positions and the exhausted 5th had to withdraw.

Prior to the February attack, the Allies had never bombed the monastery because of its religious significance. But they changed their minds that month, feeling that they could no longer allow the enemy to use it for observing the movement of the 5th's troops on the slopes below. It was later learned that the Germans had also respected the monastery's significance and had never placed troops in it, leaving it to the monks who lived there.

SMASHING THE GUSTAV LINE ▪ Though all the attacks thus far had failed, the Gustav Line was fated to be soon overrun. By the dawn of 1944, General Eisenhower had left the Italian campaign to take on the job of leading the invasion of France, which was planned for midyear. British general Harold Alexander had replaced him and was now preparing to launch an all-out assault on the Line.

The monastery at Monte Cassino was reduced to rubble by Allied bombers.

Alexander spent the first months of 1944 reducing the flow of vital equipment to the Line by continually sending bombers to attack the rail lines and roads to its north. At the same time, he strengthened the 5th and 8th armies with fresh troops and equipment.

Then, on May 11, his troops struck. This time, the Germans, with their dwindling store of equipment, could not stop them. The next days saw the attackers battle their way across the Line—with some plunging over the top of Monte Cassino—and surge toward the steel ring that had held their comrades pinned to the beaches of Anzio for so long. The men inside the ring started to fight their way out. By May 23, they had broken free and were joining the advance northward.

The Germans retreated slowly before the massive thrust, fighting for every foot of ground they surrendered. But, again, the Allies could not be stopped. Rome fell to them on June 4. Later that month, they crossed the Arno River. By August, they had arrived at the Gothic Line, a system of defenses that the Germans had established across the width of northern Italy. The Line stood in their way until it broke in October.

They continued pressing onward, only to be stopped again when winter set in and brought the fighting of 1944 to an end. The Allied troops now held most of Italy. The rest of the country would fall to them in early 1945.

But, by the close of 1944, the attention of the world had shifted away from the troops in Italy. It was focused elsewhere—on France. It had been focused there for six months, ever since June 6—D-Day.

An Italian woman sits in front of her home, which was demolished in the fierce fighting that took place as the Allies pushed north in May 1944.

TWO:
OPERATION
OVERLORD

To tell the full story of D-Day, we must go back to 1942, in the first months after America entered the war.

British and U.S. military leaders met in April of that year, and agreed to develop plans for an invasion of Western Europe. Calling it *Operation Roundup,* they hoped it could be launched in 1943. The aim was to land troops on the coast of France and then send them attacking east to Germany.

The leaders also began work on plans for an invasion that could take place even earlier, in that very year of 1942. Both plans were meant to help the Soviet Union, which lay beyond Poland to the east of Germany. The country had been under attack by Hitler since 1941. It was now so battered that Britain and America feared it would abandon the war unless they came to its aid by hitting Germany from the west.

The plan for the 1942 invasion was soon cast aside as unworkable. It was abandoned because the U.S. and British troops did not yet have all the equipment and training needed for such a giant effort.

Then Operation Roundup was put aside because the British insisted that the French west coast was too well fortified

British ports filled with U.S. ships and troops in preparation for the invasion of German-held France.

by the Germans for the invasion to succeed. It was replaced by a British plan to hit Germany from another direction—by invading North Africa and defeating the enemy troops there. This would open the way for a crossing of the Mediterranean Sea to southern France, where the beaches were not as heavily defended as those on the west coast. As a result, the invasion of North Africa was launched in November 1942, and was followed by the invasions of Sicily and Italy.

Roundup, however, was not long forgotten. President Franklin Roosevelt and British prime minister Winston Churchill held a series of meetings in 1943. At the first, which took place in North Africa in January, the two decided that western France, even though heavily defended, should be invaded as early as possible in 1944. They discussed the invasion at the sessions that followed and then informed Soviet premier Joseph Stalin of the plan during a December meeting with him at Teheran, Iran.

The news pleased the Soviet leader. By then, his armies were beginning to drive the Germans out of his country. Once the invasion was launched, Hitler's armies would be hit from both the west and east. They would be doomed to defeat.

The invasion was given a new code name, *Operation Overlord*. Named as its commander was General Eisenhower.

GETTING READY FOR OVERLORD ▪ Eisenhower was given his new job in December 1943. He immediately flew to Great Britain and set up his headquarters there. On his arrival, he found that the preparations for Overlord were well under way. As soon as the invasion had been ordered, the work of planning for it had gone to a British team. The team had begun by studying a number of possible landing sites. They finally chose the beaches of Normandy on the coast of France as the best of the lot.

Normandy lay just across the English Channel from southern England and opened into a broad and flat plain. Once they fought past the enemy defenses there, the invaders would have the French interior spread out before them.

During the months that Overlord was being planned, Great Britain became a crowded military camp. Some 1.5 million U.S. troops poured into the island country and began to train for the invasion. They joined 1.75 million soldiers from Britain and its Commonwealth nations. Also on hand were more than 40,000 fighters from the countries that Hitler had conquered: France, Norway, Poland, Belgium, and Holland.

A flood of supplies, coming mainly from America, poured into Britain along with the men—everything from rifles to tanks, airplanes, and landing craft. By early 1944, a half million tons of supplies were being landed each month.

In the midst of these preparations, British shipbuilders took on a major construction project. Its goal was to avert a danger the invading troops would face when they stormed ashore and met the German defenders. The troops had to be quickly supplied with an endless stream of equipment. If that stream ran dry, they would be unable to advance into France but would be driven back into the English Channel.

There were two major seaports near the invasion site, Le Havre and Cherbourg, that could be used for the landing of supplies. But first the ports would have to be captured, and that might take days. The Allied troops dared not wait that long. This meant that the invaders would have to take their own ports along with them.

And so, 40,000 British workers got to the job of constructing giant concrete caissons—great blocks with hollow

centers. The caissons stood as tall as five-story buildings. They were to be towed across the English Channel and then sunk to form the docks for two harbors on the Normandy coast. The two ports were code-named "Mulberries."

THE WAR IN THE AIR ▪ All the while that Overlord was taking shape, British and American bombers pounded German targets around the clock. Britain's Royal Air Force handled the night attacks on the nation's cities. The U.S. 8th and 9th air forces took on the day raids because their planes were designed for daylight bombing. Their targets were enemy war factories and oil fields. Behind the incessant air assaults were two purposes: to help defeat Germany by breaking the spirit of its people, and to help make the coming invasion easier by reducing the enemy's production of war materials.

The daylight raids did some good in 1943 but cost the Americans dearly. For example, in October the 8th Air Force sent 291 B-17 Flying Fortresses on a raid on the giant ball-bearing plant at Schweinfurt, Germany. The raid turned into the most vicious battle in the history of the U.S. Air Force. Swarms of German fighters hurled themselves at the attackers. Some flew straight in among the bombers. Others hit from the side with rockets and cannon shells. Still others roared in above the Fortresses and dumped bomb-carrying parachutes on them. One B-17 after another spun earthward. Others, though ripped open by the enemy fire, stubbornly flew on to their target.

One Fortress slammed head-on into a German fighter. The fighter exploded and crashed. But the B-17, seeming ready to break apart at any moment, managed to stay aloft. It made its bombing run and then miraculously limped all the way back to its base in England.

American M-4 tanks, B-17 bombers, and huge stockpiles of communications and railway equipment were among the supplies that poured into Britain in the months leading up to the invasion.

The raid, which interrupted Schweinfurt's ball-bearing production for just six weeks, cost the 8th sixty bombers and six hundred lives.

The raids proved so costly because the U.S. fighter planes could not carry enough fuel to escort and protect the bombers all the way to the targets. The German fighter planes would wait for the Americans just beyond the point where the escorts had to turn for home. Then the lumbering bombers became their easy prey.

For a time, it seemed that every U.S. bomber in Europe might be wiped out. But matters improved in early 1944 when the long-range P-47 and P-51 fighters arrived on the scene. They were able to escort the bombers for greater distances—sometimes clear to the target areas—and then battle the German planes that came up to meet the attack.

Eisenhower began 1944 by ordering the 8th Air Force to concentrate on destroying Germany's Luftwaffe (air force) and airplane production. Protected by their long-range fighters, the 8th's bombers pounded enemy airfields, aircraft factories, and oil refineries to dust. At the same time, the British continued their night attacks. As a result, Germany lost most of its power to defend itself from the air by the time of the invasion. Hundreds of its planes had been destroyed in the air and on the ground. There was not enough fuel left to get many of those that remained into the air.

Two months before the invasion, Eisenhower set the U.S. planes to attacking rail lines and bridges in France and Belgium. Then he had them strike at enemy airfields located within 130 miles of the Normandy beaches. All this was meant to hamper the Germans in sending men and planes to meet his troops on the day of the invasion, a day the general was calling D-Day.

American A-20 attack bombers over Normandy. In the final weeks before the invasion, Allied air raids pounded the German defenses.

THREE: D-DAY

Once Normandy was chosen, the Overlord planners had to pick a date for the invasion. Two conditions were required for the right date. First, there had to be a moon; paratroopers were to drop behind the enemy lines on the night before the landing, and they needed the moonlight to see their jump zones. Second, there had to be a rising tide, so that the landing craft could bring the invaders up close to the shore without becoming stuck in the sand.

There were only three days a month when the moon and tide together provided these conditions. One such period came in early June, and Eisenhower chose the fifth for the invasion. But no one could be sure that the often stormy English Channel would allow a landing on any given day. In case a change had to be made to another time, the invasion date was named D-Day. The next days were to be called D-plus-1, D-plus-2, and so on.

Late in May, the Allied troops began massing in camps along the British coast facing France. Looming on all sides were the transports, supply ships, and warships that would take them across the Channel—in all, some 5,300 vessels.

U.S. troops land at Omaha Beach under heavy German fire. The Normandy invasion was the largest amphibious landing in history.

Eisenhower moved his headquarters to the city of Portsmouth, a major jump-off spot for Overlord.

Everything and everyone was ready to go. But then a storm rolled out of the Atlantic Ocean and began whipping the Channel with fierce winds and a hard rain.

EISENHOWER'S LAST-MINUTE DECISION ▪ On Sunday, June 4, a deeply troubled Eisenhower paced his headquarters. He knew the surf at Normandy would be boiling in this wild weather. Any attempt to land troops there would meet with disaster. Just hours before, in the hope that the storm might soon pass, he had ordered the invasion pushed back a day—to Tuesday, June 6.

Now, with the storm still raging, he was wondering if he should delay until June 19, when the next rising tide was due at Normandy. But then weatherman Captain James Stagg arrived with hopeful news. He had just detected signs that the weather would clear for a few hours just before June 6.

Stagg's news drove Eisenhower to one of his most difficult decisions in the war. Should he wait or go ahead? Either way, the risks were great. If he chose Tuesday and the storm returned, he would be dooming Overlord to failure.

But it would be equally disastrous to delay the assault again and then have the weather clear. His troops were primed for action and ready to go. If they were made to wait until the nineteenth, their fighting edge would surely be dulled.

The general made his decision just before dawn on June 5. He met with his staff members and discussed the problem with them. Finally, he asked how long they thought the troops could be made to wait without endangering their spirit if he ordered another delay. No one could answer.

Eisenhower nodded and said: "Okay. We'll go."

General Eisenhower gives final orders to paratroopers who will lead the assault on German positions. Having led Allied forces in North Africa, Sicily, and Italy, he was given supreme command over the Allied armies that would invade Normandy.

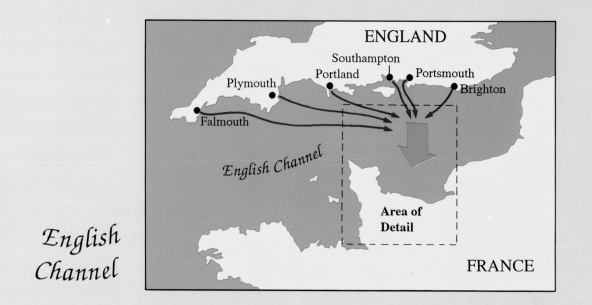

ENGLAND

Southampton
Portland
Plymouth
Portsmouth
Brighton

Falmouth

English Channel

Area of
Detail

FRANCE

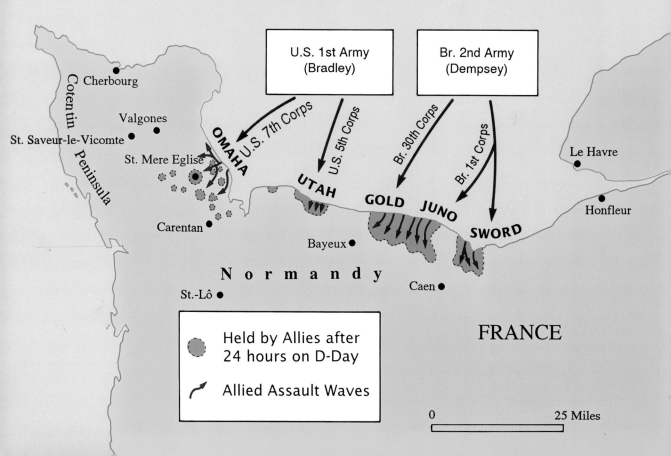

English
Channel

Cherbourg

Cotentin

Valgones

St. Saveur-le-Vicomte

Peninsula

St. Mere Eglise

OMAHA

U.S. 7th Corps

U.S. 1st Army
(Bradley)

U.S. 5th Corps

Br. 2nd Army
(Dempsey)

Br. 30th Corps

Br. 1st Corps

Le Havre

Carentan

UTAH

GOLD

JUNO

SWORD

Honfleur

Bayeux

N o r m a n d y

Caen

St.-Lô

FRANCE

Held by Allies after
24 hours on D-Day

Allied Assault Waves

0   25 Miles

British, Canadian, and U.S. paratroopers took off late at night on June 5, flew to France, and plunged through the darkness to points behind the German defenses. The British and Canadians belonged to the 6th Airborne Division, and the Americans to the 82nd and 101st airborne divisions. Once on the ground, they destroyed bridges, cut telephone lines, and took over roads—all to keep the Germans from quickly sending reinforcements to help defend the Normandy shores.

While the troopers worked, the invasion fleet was crossing the Channel. As a gray dawn broke, the ships moved up to their destination, a shoreline that ran from east to west for over fifty miles. Just beyond its eastern end stood the port of Le Havre. To the west, the land jutted outward to form the Cotentin Peninsula.

The Germans, knowing an invasion would come one day, had spent months building defensive positions all along the French coast. Now, Overlord's fleet of warships opened fire on the Normandy positions. Then the transports began releasing their landing craft. The first of the men due to land started the wave-tossed journey to shore.

The troops were divided into two forces—the American 1st Army led by Lieutenant General Omar N. Bradley, and the British 2nd Army under Lieutenant General Sir Miles Dempsey. In command of both armies was General Sir Bernard Montgomery.

Overlord's planners had divided the invasion site into five "beaches": Sword, Juno, Gold, Omaha, and Utah. The British 2nd, which included a number of Canadian units, moved in to attack Sword, Juno, and Gold beaches. The Americans had the job of taking Omaha and Utah beaches.

Sword, Juno, Gold, and Utah were lightly defended because Hitler had expected the invasion to come at the distant port city of Calais and had placed most of his troops there. Though the German resistance was sharp, it could not stop the invaders from working their way through the shore defenses—gun emplacements, barbed-wire entanglements, and steel beams that were embedded in concrete and pointed seaward at sharp angles. Everyone was ashore by late afternoon.

The fiercest fighting took place at Omaha Beach, where the shore ran up to a line of 150-foot-high bluffs. Here, the coast was more heavily defended. As soon as the landing craft were sighted, rockets and artillery shells began raining down on them from the bluffs. Machine guns all along the bluffs unleashed a withering fire.

Instantly, there was chaos among the landing craft. Some exploded as the shells hit them. Some reached the surf and dropped their front ramps, only to have the men inside killed by the machine-gun fire before they could rush down to the water. Some craft, fearful of the deadly fire, released their passengers too soon; the troops plunged into deep water and drowned when their heavy backpacks pulled them beneath the surface. But other craft plowed up onto the beach and returned the enemy fire with their machine guns.

The men who were not hit while aboard the landing craft found death everywhere on entering the water. Everywhere, their fellow soldiers were dropping. Everywhere, the surf was awash with bodies. Everywhere, there were the cries of the wounded. Numbed by the crash of the guns, they struggled ahead, certain that they would die in the next seconds.

Then, on reaching the shore, they found themselves stopped by barbed-wire entanglements and by those sharply

At Utah Beach, U.S. soldiers help others to shore after their landing craft was sunk by German fire.

angled steel beams. They lay helplessly at the water's edge while demolition teams inched forward to place dynamite charges that would blast aside the obstacles. Many of the demolition men died when they stepped on buried land mines.

The gray sky turned black with smoke. The battleships offshore sent their shells hurtling into the bluffs. Destroyers, firing nonstop, ran in so close to the beach that they risked going aground. Bombers streaked above the German positions. But, afraid to hit the Americans below, most dropped their loads harmlessly behind the bluffs.

Throughout the morning, General Bradley watched the battle from the deck of the battleship *Augusta*. He grimly listened to the reports of how his troops were dying. He wondered whether he should pull the men off the beach.

But on the beach itself, the demolition teams were at last blowing pathways through the barbed wire and steel beams. Officers were starting to move their men. One inched his men forward by crawling on all fours while poking the sand with a knife to find the hidden land mines.

By afternoon, Bradley learned that things were changing in favor of his troops. Somehow, they were moving through the deadly enemy fire and beyond the barbed wire. Aided by the tanks and armored vehicles that were pouring ashore, they were fanning out all along the beach.

At dusk, both Bradley and General Dempsey could report to Eisenhower that the invasion was succeeding. Some 55,000 men were ashore, preparing for a push inland.

But the invasion was a victory being won at a terrible cost for the Allies. Ten thousand men lay dead at Normandy. The American losses totaled six thousand.

D-Day was at an end.

American soldiers injured in the assault on Omaha Beach await evacuation to a field hospital.

D-Day had given the Allies a foothold in Normandy. Now they had to accomplish two tasks before they could hope to break out of Normandy and move deep into France.

First, they had to expand their foothold so that the enemy would be unable to drive them back into the Channel. Second, they had to bring in the men and supplies still in England—all the equipment and manpower that would be needed for the thrust into the French interior.

PREPARING TO BREAK OUT ▪ To expand their foothold, the troops fanned out in two directions. The British 2nd Army moved toward the city of Caen, some twenty miles inland. The Americans attacked Cotentin Peninsula to seal off the troops there from the rest of the German defenders. By June 17, some of the U.S. units had advanced clear across the base of the peninsula.

Back at the invasion site, the buildup of supplies and men took shape quickly. The first week after D-Day saw 300,000 men and 54,000 vehicles arrive aboard landing craft that brought them right up to the shore. At the same time,

Two French children survey the ruins of the Normandy town of St.-Lô, which fell to the Allies on July 18.

the concrete caissons that would form the two "Mulberry" harbors were towed across the Channel. One was meant for the British. The other was placed at Omaha Beach for the Americans. Both were ready for use by mid-month.

Though carried out at a furious pace, the job of landing the supplies and men on the beach sands was difficult and time-consuming. The Mulberries, with their regular docks, promised to make things go more quickly. But nature gave them no chance to be of use. On June 19, a new storm struck Normandy. It completely destroyed the U.S. Mulberry and sent the Americans back to the beach landings. The British Mulberry suffered some damage but was soon repaired.

The storm was also a misfortune for the men in the field. It stalled their progress for four days and gave the Germans time to rush more reinforcements into the area.

When good weather returned, General Bradley sent troops to take Cherbourg on Cotentin Peninsula. Because of the loss of the U.S. Mulberry, the city's harbor was desperately needed for the supply landings. Moving quickly, the Americans cap-

FIELD MARSHAL ERWIN ROMMEL

Called the "Desert Fox" because of his brilliant tactics in North Africa, Rommel commanded German troops in western France at the time of the Normandy invasion. However, after a band of German officers attempted to assassinate Hitler in 1944, Rommel came under suspicion as one of the plotters. Given the choice of committing suicide or enduring a trial, he chose to end his life by taking poison.

tured Cherbourg on June 27, only to find that the enemy had demolished the harbor as they approached. A month of rebuilding would pass before the first Allied ships docked there.

The move on Cherbourg had been swift, but the same could not be said for the British march toward Caen. A stubborn enemy repeatedly slowed the thrust. It was not until July 9 that Caen finally fell.

The British were not alone in experiencing difficulty. Bradley's troops were advancing from the base of Cotentin to the town of St.-Lô, and were inching along at a snail's pace. Two things kept them at a crawl. First, they were being mauled by the enemy's superb Tiger tanks, which could hit a target from the amazing distance of four thousand yards. Second, there was the Normandy countryside itself.

Normandy was a farming area of small fields. Separating them were thick rows of earthern mounds topped by high hedges of bushes and tangled vines. Called hedgerows, they had been there for centuries, and they now served the Germans well as Bradley's men tried to cross the fields. From behind the mounds, enemy riflemen easily cut down the oncoming troops. The U.S. tanks, on trying to climb over the mounds, found themselves mired in the thick hedges. Any tank that reached the top became a fine target for antitank fire.

Acting on the advice of an enlisted soldier, Bradley solved the hedgerow problem. He had the steel beams that had guarded the invasion beaches fashioned into sharp blades that were then attached to the fronts of his tanks. The blades, working like giant scythes, began to rip through the hedges. Immediately, the U.S. advance gained speed. St.-Lô fell to the general on July 18.

Once Caen and St.-Lô toppled, the Allies stood ready to strike at the heart of France. By now, there were more than 1.4 million Allied troops ashore. And, by now, Bradley had been placed in command of what was called the U.S. 12th Army Group. Under him were two armies—his old 1st (now led by Lieutenant General Courtney Hodges) and the 3rd. The 3rd was a newly created outfit and was headed by the fierce Lieutenant General George S. Patton, who had fought in North Africa and Sicily.

SWEEPING ACROSS FRANCE ▪ The breakout from Normandy began on July 25. The rest of 1944 saw the Allies sweep through France and into Belgium, Holland, and Luxembourg.

Thrusting out from St.-Lô, the U.S. 1st Army fought its way to Coutances, taking the town on July 28. General Patton's army then charged past and spent the next three weeks in a circling move. His first targets were the cities of Avranches and Nantes. From Nantes, he swung back toward Normandy

Steel beams sharpened into blades (inset) allowed U.S. tanks to slice through the hedgerows that crisscrossed the Normandy countryside.

GENERAL OMAR N. BRADLEY

A quiet, scholarly-looking man, Bradley commanded the U.S. 1st Army during the fiercely contested landing at Omaha Beach. Later, he was appointed the chief of all the American ground troops in France.

and headed for Argentan. When he arrived there in mid-August, his dash had formed almost all of a giant, oval-shaped pocket. Caught inside it were four enemy divisions.

Patton now planned to close the pocket and prevent a German escape by taking nearby Falaise. But Bradley told him that Falaise was in the British sector. The town was to be taken by a Canadian force, while he was to probe deeper into France. Angry at not being allowed to finish his job, Patton set out on a path that would finally take him into Germany.

On August 15, a new U.S. army, the 7th, arrived on the scene and invaded the lightly defended southern coast of France. The invasion, which had long been planned to assist the sweep across France, sent the 7th and seven divisions of Free French fighters marching north along the Rhône River. In September, they linked up with Patton near the city of Dijon and pressed on toward Germany with him.

The British and Canadians broke out of Normandy along two fronts. Some Canadian units thrust inland to Falaise and, trapping thousands of Germans, closed the pocket that Patton had formed. Others moved up the French west coast. They spent September taking the port cities along their route, at last reaching Calais near the Belgium border. All the ports were needed for the landing of Allied supplies.

British troops traveled inland of the Canadians and captured the city of Amiens on August 31. Then they readied themselves to cross over into Belgium.

General Hodges and the U.S. 1st Army were also sweeping north. At first, the general seemed to be heading for the French capital, Paris, which had been occupied by the Germans since 1940. But then he swung away and marched farther north to another city, Soissons.

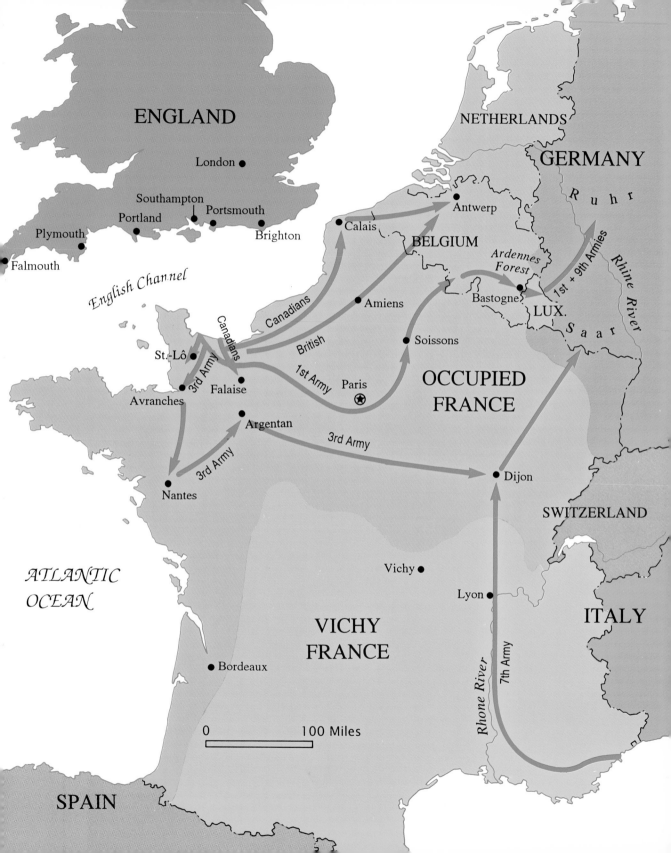

The honor of taking Paris went to General Charles de Gaulle, the leader of the French forces fighting alongside the Allies. His men, accompanied by a unit from the 1st, marched into the capital on August 25 and set it free without bloodshed. The German occupation troops there had fled.

THE FINAL MONTHS OF 1944 ▪ The Allies advanced swiftly through France for two reasons. First, on leaving Normandy, they entered open country and were able to move at great speeds. Second, the enemy troops were vastly outnumbered. Though fighting back courageously, they were forced to retreat before the surging Allied tide. The retreat took them toward the German border, where they would stage a stubborn defense of their nation.

In late August, the British and Canadians who had come up the French west coast at last made their way into Belgium. They immediately captured the city of Antwerp. Its giant harbor became all-important to the Allies for the landing of their supplies.

GENERAL CHARLES DE GAULLE

De Gaulle led the French forces who participated in the Allied drive across France. In 1944, he established a provisional government for France after four years of occupation by the Germans. In the late 1950s and then the 1960s, de Gaulle served as president of France.

The 1st Army also marched into Belgium after capturing Soissons, north of Paris. Hodges's troops then swung east into Luxembourg. Both nations bordered Germany.

The British and Americans now set about invading Germany itself. They launched a massive ground and airborne effort in September to cross one of the nation's major rivers, the Rhine. The attempt failed when troops at a key crossing point were defeated. Had the attempt succeeded, the Allies would have entered open country that led into the heart of Germany.

September, however, did see the 1st Army enter Germany from Belgium and Luxembourg and begin to inch toward the Ruhr district, a major industrial area that produced much of Hitler's coal and iron. Up against enemy troops who were no longer retreating but savagely defending their endangered country, the Americans paid dearly in lives for every foot of ground they won. Then, with the U.S. 9th Army (which had recently arrived in Europe), the 1st battled its way to the Ruhr as December approached.

GENERAL DIETRICH VON CHOLITZ

Von Cholitz was the commander of the German troops occupying Paris. When Hitler learned that the Allies were approaching Paris, he ordered the general to set fire to the city and destroy it. Von Cholitz loved the French capital, its long history, and its art treasures. He ignored Hitler's order and turned the city over to the Allies on their arrival there.

Far to the south, the U.S. 3rd and 7th armies were likewise across the German border and were closing in on another of the nation's vital industrial areas, the Saar region.

By December, the Allied front line extended miles down the German frontier, from Holland and Belgium on the north to the Saar region in the south. And, by that month, the worst winter in fifty years had settled over Europe, bringing with it heavy snows and icy winds.

It was then the Germans struck back with a surprise blow that Hitler believed would end the war.

FIVE:
THE BATTLE OF
THE BULGE

The attack came on December 16. Without warning, a massive enemy force burst out of Germany and hurled itself at the U.S. troops stationed along the Belgium and Luxembourg borders. The assault marked the start of an offensive that the Americans soon nicknamed the "Battle of the Bulge" because of the deep bend it carved into their lines.

Despite the heavy losses he had suffered since Normandy, Hitler had somehow massed three armies for the attack. They were under orders to plunge across Belgium and take Antwerp. If successful, they would drive a giant wedge between the British and U.S. troops in northern Europe and capture the chief port for the landing of Allied supplies. This, Hitler believed, would soon bring the war to an end in his favor. The Allies, with their forces split and without supplies from Antwerp, would become too discouraged to fight on.

The attack was Hitler's idea alone. His chief generals thought it foolish, telling themselves that the Allies would never quit but would fight back, retake Antwerp, and march on to Germany. The generals, however, dared not argue with the dictator. For them, his word was law.

Hitler's idea may have been foolish, but he chose the place for the attack well. He secretly massed his three armies along a stretch of the Belgian border that extended south for eighty-five miles into Luxembourg. It lay about midway between the Ruhr and Saar battlegrounds and was the quietest and most lightly manned area on the Allied front. Defending it were outfits waiting for the winter to pass before going into action—in all, just six divisions from General Hodges's 1st Army. Three were veteran combat units at rest after fighting in the Ruhr. The others were "green" divisions, outfits new to the war and yet to serve in battle. The rest of the 1st was still in the Ruhr.

The border was lightly defended because it ran through the Forest of the Ardennes. The Allies felt certain that, should Hitler ever try an attack of some sort, he would not attempt it here. The thick woods, especially in the winter snow, would prove too difficult an obstacle for his tanks. Further, the Allies believed the dictator no longer had the strength left for a major attack—not after having lost more than a million men in the fighting so far.

THE FIRST DAYS OF BATTLE ▪ A heavy fog coated the snow-covered border at dawn that December 16 as the U.S. troops began stirring and getting ready for another day. All was silent at 5:29 A.M. One minute later, the quiet was shattered for days to come.

The attack opened with an artillery barrage that tore the U.S. lines apart for forty-five minutes. Then, when it ended, the battered Americans picked up a host of new sounds—the harsh rattle of tanks coming through the trees and the shouts of German infantrymen. The first of 250,000 enemy soldiers and their armor began to pour across the border.

M-4 tanks lined up in the snow near St.-Vith, a region that was at the center of the German advance into Belgium.

Stunned by the size and ferocity of the attack, the U.S. units reacted in different ways. Some retreated in confusion as the enemy rolled in on them. Some stood their ground, only to be overrun. Units stationed just behind the lines came rushing forward to help. Some were then hurled back by the onslaught. Some were captured.

Adding to the chaos was a small band of English-speaking Germans dressed in American uniforms. They sneaked in behind the U.S. units to cause as much trouble as possible. They spread rumors of German victories. They removed or changed road signs. On meeting reinforcements looking for the front lines, they sent them in the wrong direction.

There was more chaos when the Americans realized that a disguised enemy was in their midst. The troops became suspicious of anyone in a U.S. uniform. Valuable time was lost whenever they came upon someone they did not know. The stranger was made to answer questions on topics that only an American was likely to know, such as the names of baseball teams. He was in danger until he gave the right answers.

The first hours, and then days, of the offensive saw two of Hitler's three armies move with lightning speed. The army at the southern end of the front, the German 7th, overran a series of villages and headed for one of the most important target cities in the offensive, Bastogne. At the center of the front, the 5th Panzer (tank) Army swept in on the city of St.-Vith and then joined the run to Bastogne. Within two days, the two armies had pushed thirty miles into Belgium.

So swiftly did the Germans move that some did not bother to take prisoners. A panzer unit one day captured 125 Americans near the village of Malmédy. Rather than imprisoning them, the panzer commander herded them together and had his men gun them down. Eighty-five died instantly. Their comrades saved themselves by falling and pretending to be dead.

All this did not mean that the Americans were beaten everywhere. A U.S. victory came when the enemy army at the northern end of the front thought it would have an easy time with the "green" 99th Division. But the Americans, though new to battle, did not flee when hit. Instead, they dug in along a nearby ridge of hills. There, joined by veteran fighters from the 2nd Division, they fought off four days of savage assaults and caused the attack at their end of the front to fail.

Another American victory came at Bastogne.

THE STAND AT BASTOGNE ▪ For the Germans, the city was a vital target on their march to Antwerp. It had to be captured because seven major roadways fanned out from it. They were needed to move men and equipment quickly and keep the offensive rolling at top speed. Given the job of taking Bastogne were the 5th Panzer and 7th armies.

General Eisenhower, at his headquarters in France, recognized the importance of Bastogne to the German advance. The city was defended by a few units of the U.S. 9th Armored Division. The general immediately sent two divisions to join them. The 101st Airborne hurried in from its camp in France while the 10th Armored, which belonged to Patton's 3rd Army, came up from the Saar. Both were in place and had formed a defensive ring around the city by the time the Germans arrived on December 19.

On that same day, Eisenhower completed plans for crushing the entire offensive. He began stationing troops along the northern edge of the advance and directly in its path. Moved into position were troops that had been retreating, reserve troops from France and distant points in Belgium, and units of the 1st Army in the Ruhr. As they were taking their posts, Patton's 3rd Army began to rush up from the Saar.

Eisenhower's plan called for Patton to knife in behind the German frontline force at Bastogne and separate it from its men to the rear. Then he was to move on and join the Allied troops now massing to the front and side of the enemy march. Together, they would press in on the Germans and drive them out of Belgium.

But Eisenhower faced a disturbing question. The men at Bastogne had to hold the city until the 3rd arrived. Should it be captured, the job of retaking it would be costly in lives and would delay the work of stopping the entire offensive. And so: Could the badly outnumbered troops there hang on for the several days Patton would need to reach them?

When the Germans came up to Bastogne, they spent four days vainly trying to smash through its ring of defenses. On the fourth day, December 22, Hitler sent a special order to his commanding general at the city, Heinz Kokott. The dictator had learned that Patton was speeding north from the Saar. He instructed Kokott to stop trying to take Bastogne by force but to seek a fast surrender from the American commander in the city—Brigadier General Anthony McAuliffe of the 101st Airborne.

Kokott immediately sent two officers and two enlisted men into the U.S. lines under a white flag. They carried a

U.S. Army engineers search for mines in the Ardennes. Snow added to the danger by hiding visual clues and weakening the signals from the magnetic mine detectors.

message that urged the outnumbered McAuliffe to avoid further bloodshed and surrender. On being met by American soldiers, they were escorted to a nearby command post. Their message was telephoned to McAuliffe inside Bastogne.

McAuliffe listened to the message and then gave a one-word reply that instantly became famous throughout the Allied world: "Nuts."

The foursome departed in silence, and the battle for the city continued. On Christmas Day, the Germans burst through the American lines at one point, only to find that they had stumbled into a trap. Airborne troops, hidden in the snow, began to drop the advancing foot soldiers, while an antitank battalion blasted the enemy tanks, destroying seventeen. Badly mauled, the enemy retreated.

Christmas Day marked a turning point in the German fortunes. Not only did they fail to take Bastogne, but the leading units in Patton's 3rd Army arrived on the scene as well. The general began to spear in behind the enemy front-line troops on his way north to join the forces now in place and ready to put an end to the German offensive.

The final days of December saw the Allies stop the advance wherever they met it and begin to drive the Germans out of Belgium. The drive would continue through the first weeks of 1945. By February, the last of the Germans would be back over their own border. The offensive cost them almost 120,000 men—12,652 killed, 57,000 injured, and 50,000 taken prisoner. The Americans suffered 8,500 killed and 46,000 wounded. Some 21,000 were missing or taken prisoner.

The Battle of the Bulge was at an end. To come in the next weeks of 1945 was the final battle for Germany, a struggle that would mark the end of the war in Europe.

General Patton pins a Distinguished Service Cross on General Anthony McAuliffe, assistant division commander of the 101st Airborne and head of the troops defending Bastogne. Patton, shown here wearing his trademark pearl-handled revolver, was known to his troops as "Blood and Guts" because of his eagerness for battle.

SIX: FIGHTING THE PACIFIC WAR

To understand the fighting in the Pacific during 1944, we must go back to 1942 when the military leaders in Washington, D.C., began to develop a master plan for the defeat of Japan. It called for the Pacific forces to undertake two campaigns that would close in on the island nation from two different directions.

The first campaign, which was to be commanded by General Douglas MacArthur, would strike from Australia and advance north to retake the Philippine Islands, which had fallen to the Japanese in 1942. Once the Philippines were won, MacArthur would press on to Japan.

Admiral Chester W. Nimitz was to lead the second campaign. He would attack from the east, from out in the Pacific Ocean. His mission: to capture a string of Japanese-held islands and then strike at Japan itself.

WITH MACARTHUR IN THE PACIFIC ▪ General MacArthur spent 1942 and 1943 invading a cluster of enemy-held islands immediately north of Australia. Looming as barriers on the route to the Philippines, they were New Guinea, the Solomon Is-

The guns of the U.S.S. *Pennsylvania* pound shore installations on Guam in July 1944.

lands, and New Britain. By the end of 1943, after months of vicious fighting, his troops had captured the main islands in the Solomon group, among them Guadalcanal and Bougainville. And his forces had surrounded New Britain and had ended its role as a major Japanese supply base.

Most important of all, by the opening of 1944, they had won control of more than half of 319,000-square-mile New Guinea, the largest of their targets.

The new year saw MacArthur's men struggle toward the western tip of the giant island, where they would be able to embark for the Philippines. They fought off heavy enemy counterattacks all along the way. At last, in August and September, they not only reached their destination but went beyond it to the island of Morotai.

Morotai lay just 250 miles from the southernmost tip of the Philippines. MacArthur now readied his troops and ships to fulfill a promise he had made in early 1942. At that time, the general had been in command of the troops defending the Philippines against the invading Japanese. He had vowed to remain at his post until the very end of the fighting, but had then been ordered by President Roosevelt to escape to Australia and take command of the Allied forces in the South Pacific. On reaching Australia, he had broadcast a simple promise to the Philippine people, whose country was doomed to fall to the Japanese in a few more weeks: ''I shall return.''

"ISLAND HOPPING" WITH NIMITZ ▪ Admiral Nimitz began his advance on Japan in November 1943, when he sailed his fleet one thousand miles to the northeast of the Solomons and moved in among the Gilbert Islands. There, his marines stormed ashore at the island of Makin and a tiny atoll about

105 miles away, Tarawa. The fight to take Makin, which was defended by eight hundred Japanese, was easily won. But the same could not be said of Tarawa. Some five thousand Japanese were entrenched there. They claimed the lives of more than two thousand marines before surrendering.

As he sailed on from the Gilberts, Nimitz employed a two-part strategy that became known as "island hopping." First, it called for him to take only certain islands while bypassing others of lesser importance. Japanese outposts on those that were bypassed withered away because they could no longer be supplied by ships from their homeland.

Second, on capturing an island, Nimitz turned it into an air base for the bombing of the next targets on his list. The admiral always opened his attack on an island with a heavy air bombardment from his carriers and the bases he had established on previously captured islands. Only when a bombardment had thoroughly "softened" the target island did he send his men ashore. Often, when the air attacks completely destroyed an island's air bases and made it impossible for the Japanese to strike back, he moved on without making a landing.

In the first nine months of 1944, Nimitz probed steadily toward Japan. Chief among the islands he struck were:

Kwajalein ▪ Located in the Marshall Islands north of the Gilberts, this atoll (the world's largest) fell to 40,000 Army troops in February after suffering one of the heaviest air bombings in the Pacific fighting. The Japanese lost almost five thousand lives in the invasion.

Truk ▪ Lying in the Caroline Islands to the west of the Marshalls, Truk served as the home of a giant Japanese naval

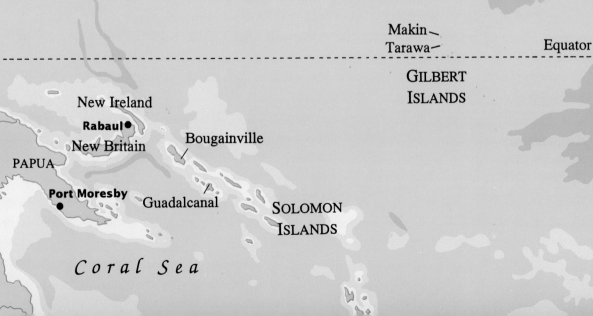

MIDWAY
ISLANDS

Wake

P A C I F I C   O C E A N

MARIANA
ISLANDS

Saipan

Guam

Kwajalein —

MARSHALL
ISLANDS

CAROLINE ISLANDS
Truk

Makin —
Tarawa —

Equator

GILBERT
ISLANDS

New Ireland

Rabaul●

New Britain

Bougainville

PAPUA

Port Moresby
●

Guadalcanal

SOLOMON
ISLANDS

Coral Sea

and supply base. In February, Nimitz sent an armada of planes to level the base. The attack proved devastating for the Japanese. It destroyed 250 of their planes and sent 41 ships to the bottom. The base was rendered useless, and Truk was left in the admiral's wake.

Saipan and Guam ▪ These islands were located in the Mariana group to the north of the Carolines. On reaching Saipan and taking it in July, Nimitz had come so far north that his bombers could now reach Japan itself. Guam, which the Japanese had wrested from a small U.S force in 1941, was successfully invaded by Army and Marine troops in July.

The invasion of Saipan alarmed Japan's military leaders. Nimitz was too close to their homeland for comfort. They immediately ordered a naval force out to drive him away from Saipan. It proved to be a disastrous move on their part. When their warships steamed up to the admiral's fleet on June 19, his torpedo planes and submarines sent three Japanese carriers to the bottom. The Japanese also suffered the loss of more than four hundred aircraft. The engagement went down in the history of the war as the Battle of the Philippine Sea.

After Saipan and Guam, Nimitz did not venture closer to Japan. Rather, on orders from Washington, he turned southwest and struck the heavily defended Palau Islands in September. They were located near the Philippines, and he moved on them to support MacArthur's upcoming invasion of the island nation.

A U.S. infantry unit on Guam in July 1944.

THE PHILIPPINES INVADED ▪ MacArthur planned to retake the Philippines by first invading Mindanao, the nation's southernmost island. He then intended to build air bases there to

support his thrust north to Luzon. It was the largest island in the Philippine chain and the home of the national capital, Manila.

But Admiral William Halsey, the commander of the U.S. 3rd Fleet, suggested a change in the plan. In September, his carriers struck at Japanese bases in the Philippines to keep them from sending ships and aircraft to repel the Nimitz attack on the Palau Islands. Halsey's pilots returned from raids on the island of Leyte to say that they had met scant enemy gunfire there. This convinced the admiral that Leyte, which lay between Mindanao and Luzon, was lightly defended. He advised that it replace Mindanao as the invasion target.

MacArthur liked the idea. The result: His forces struck the east coast of Leyte on October 20. The general followed them up to the beaches, wading through the surf after his landing craft went aground on a rock. Once ashore, he made an announcement that quickly spread among the Philippine people. It was as simple as his promise of 1942:

"I have returned."

General MacArthur wades ashore at Lyete in his greatest moment of 1944. "I have returned," he told the people of the Philippines.

ADMIRAL WILLIAM "BULL" HALSEY

It was Halsey, the commander of the U.S. 3rd Fleet, who suggested that the Philippines be invaded via Leyte rather than Mindanao. Many people thought he was nicknamed "Bull" because of his aggressive battle tactics. Such was not the case. The nickname dated back to the admiral's college football days when he was known for "bulling" his way through the opposing line.

The invaders landed at four points on the Leyte coast that October 20. At only one did they meet a strong enemy resistance. Within three days, they had established beachheads and were beginning to move inland. Some speared directly across the island. Others swung toward its southern shores. Still others turned toward its northern coast.

This is not to say that the Japanese did not battle back savagely. Three naval task forces sped to Leyte in an attempt to drive the invaders back out to sea. For the Japanese, it was an effort that proved as disastrous as the Battle of the Philippine Sea. Driven off by U.S. warships and planes, the three forces lost six heavy cruisers, four light cruisers, and three battleships. In addition, many of their other ships were severely damaged.

Despite this staggering defeat, the Japanese remained determined to repel the invasion force. Their planes attacked the ships bringing supplies to the U.S. troops on land. They poured reinforcements into the town of Ormoc on Leyte's northwestern coast and sent them charging south to meet the oncoming Americans. The reinforcements and weeks of bad weather slowed the U.S. advance and caused it to drag on through November and into December.

To put an end to the flood of enemy reinforcements, MacArthur had the U.S. 77th Division sail up the eastern face of Leyte and over to the northwestern coast to attack Ormoc on December 7, the third anniversary of the assault on Pearl Harbor. The town fell to the 77th three days later. The 77th then plunged inland to meet the U.S. units moving toward the northern coast. The meeting marked the end of the strongest resistance on Leyte. The island was firmly in U.S. hands by Christmas Day.

Even before Leyte was completely his, MacArthur launched his next move. In mid-December, his troops landed at Mindoro, just off the southwestern shores of Luzon. They met only light resistance, and construction of an airfield to support the coming attack on Luzon was begun before Christmas. It took shape a mere seventy-five miles from Manila.

At the close of 1944, both MacArthur and Nimitz could look back on the year as one of great successes. The opening months of 1945 were to be fateful ones for the two men. MacArthur would land on Luzon and then bring all of the Philippines under his control. Nimitz would attack two islands close to Japan—the giant Okinawa and the tiny Iwo Jima. Both attacks would trigger some of the bloodiest fighting of the entire Pacific war.

As 1945 dawned, all the American men and women in uniform—and all the civilians at home—felt certain that the war in Europe would end sometime in the new year. The headlines told them that Hitler's forces were falling back everywhere before the Allied onslaught from the west and the Russian attack from the east. Germany could not help but soon collapse in ruins.

But the Pacific fighting brought a deep sense of dread to Americans. Just as the headlines spoke of a collapsing Germany, so did they speak of how MacArthur and Nimitz were swiftly closing in on Japan itself. They also spoke of how British forces and American-led Chinese troops were now driving the Japanese out of Burma, which the enemy had overrun in December 1941. But there were no indications that the Japanese military leaders would soon surrender and put an end to the bloodshed. There was the deep fear that the Allies would have to invade the Japanese home islands and subdue them one at a time. If so, the war would drag on for years, costing countless Japanese civilians their lives and sacrificing the lives of more than one million American, Australian, New Zealand, Chinese, and British fighters.

What the American men and women in uniform and the people at home did not know was that two terrible bombs—bearing the odd names ''Little Boy'' and ''Fat Man''—were being assembled in the New Mexico desert as part of a secret program called the Manhattan Project. When completed and used for the first time in August 1945, they would destroy the Japanese cities of Hiroshima and Nagasaki, bring Japan suddenly to its knees, and propel the world into a new and, for people everywhere, frightening era—the atomic age.

BIBLIOGRAPHY

Associated Press. *World War II: A 50th Anniversary History*. New York: Holt, 1989.

Bailey, Thomas A. *The American Pageant: A History of the Republic*. Boston: D. C. Heath, 1956.

Dolan, Edward F. *Victory in Europe: The Fall of Hitler's Germany*. New York: Franklin Watts, 1988.

Gilbert, Martin. *The Second World War: A Complete History*. New York: Holt, 1989.

Hall, John Whitney, ed. *History of the World: World War I to the Present Day*. London: Bison Books, 1988.

Lawson, Don. *The United States in World War II*. New York: Abelard-Schuman, 1963.

Manchester, William. *American Caesar: Douglas MacArthur, 1880–1964*. Boston: Little, Brown, 1978.

Morison, Samuel Eliot, and Commanger, Henry Steele. *The Growth of the American Republic, 1865–1950*, 7th ed. New York: Oxford University Press, 1980.

Pimlott, John. *The Battle of the Bulge*. London: Bison Books, 1981.

Steinberg, Rafael, and the editors of Time-Life Books. *Return to the Philippines*. Alexandria, Va.: Time-Life Books, 1979.

Sulzberger, C. L. *The American Heritage Picture History of World War II*. New York: American Heritage Publishing, 1966.

———. *The Rising Sun: The Decline and Fall of the Japanese Empire, 1936–1945*. New York: Random House, 1970.

Time Capsule/1944: A History of the Year Condensed from the Pages of Time. New York: Time-Life Books, 1967.

Young, Brigadier Peter. *D-Day*. London: Bison Books, 1981.

INDEX